PASTORAL POCKET GUIDE

FAITH AND BAPTISM

FAITH AND BAPTISM
CHURCHLEADERS
PASTORAL POCKET GUIDES

First Edition: Year 2022
Faith and Baptism (ChurchLeaders Pastoral Pocket Guides)
/ Outreach, Inc.
Paperback ISBN: 978-1-958585-06-1
eBook ISBN: 978-1-958585-07-8

CHURCHLEADERS
PRESS

Colorado Springs

CHURCHLEADERS
PASTORAL POCKET GUIDES

FAITH AND BAPTISM

Written by
John Fanella

General Editor
Matthew Lockhart

CHURCHLEADERS
PRESS

Colorado Springs

Contents

ChurchLeaders
Pastoral Pocket Guides Introduction

Be shepherds of God's flock that is under your care, watching over them—not because you must, but because you are willing, as God wants you to be; not pursuing dishonest gain, but eager to serve; not lording it over those entrusted to you, but being examples to the flock.
(1 Peter 5:2-3)

*T*he work of a shepherd is never done. One minute you're preparing a sermon and the next you're making an emergency hospital visit or planning an unexpected funeral.

When called to your common and recurring ministerial duties (such as hospital visits, weddings, baptisms, and funerals, to name a few) where do you turn for practical advice or just a couple fresh ideas?

You could spend hours online, scrolling through dozens of sites, or pull that thick, old minister's manual off your shelf. Now you can turn to these new **Pastoral Pocket Guides**, designed especially for busy pastors like you. They're quick reads, each book laser-focused on a specific area of ministry. Packed with practical guidance, tips, and tools, they'll help make taking care of your flock a little easier.

Thank you for being a willing shepherd. May God bless and guide you in your ministry!

—**Matthew Lockhart,** General Editor

1 WELCOME TO THE FAITH & BAPTISM POCKET GUIDE

*Y*ou finally have someone interested in placing their faith in Jesus Christ for the first time. Now what? What should you say? What should you do? And when should you say it and do it? Should you offer a class? Should you have them fill out a form? Should you lead them in prayer? If you do it wrong, will it be invalid? And just how much water do you need to use, anyway? Relax. Help is on the way.

Welcome to *Faith and Baptism*. This part of pastoral ministry is among the most joyful. You get to walk with people into personal faith and confirm their decision in the water of baptism, just as Jesus commanded in the great commission:

Therefore, go and make disciples of all nations, baptizing them in the name of the Father and of the Son and of the Holy Spirit, and teaching them to obey everything I have commanded you. And surely I am with you always, to the very end of the age. (Matt. 28:19-20)

In this book, we are using the word *faith* to describe the work of introducing people to salvation in Christ—as in *sharing your faith* (also called evangelism or outreach). We are using the word *baptism* to describe the act of confirming (or you could use the word *sealing*) that faith publicly through the application of water in the Name of the Trinity. What an awesome privilege we have in seeing people's lives changed by the good news of Jesus, becoming a part of the Body of Christ, and sealing that faith publicly through baptism!

We understand there are varying beliefs about baptism, even among generally like-minded evangelicals and baptizing denominations. The purpose of this handy little guide is not to address or resolve longstanding questions pertaining to baptism (e.g., Is baptism necessary for salvation and church membership? Is immersion the only proper mode? Should you baptize only believing adults?) Rather, our focus is on the practical aspects of the joyous occasion of baptizing new believers, a practice shared throughout the ages by Bible-believing Christian churches around the globe.

Have no doubt that this book is a field guide with tips and tools you can use today—all birthed out of decades in pastoral ministry in churches of all sizes. However, before we get to the practical stuff, let's celebrate some foundational beliefs that make faith and baptism so significant.

When people come to personal faith in Jesus Christ...

God gives them grace

Grace is receiving that which we do not deserve. Through faith in Jesus, God has promised to give us grace rather than the condemnation that we deserve (Romans 3:24).

God forgives all their sins

Just as water washes the body clean, so the blood of Jesus washes away all our sins. Yes, we are sinners. But in Christ, we are forgiven sinners (Ephesians 1:7).

God adopts them as his children

God's promise is much more than a courtroom promise, where we are guilty, and he acquits us. It is a family-room promise, where He adopts us as his own children. In Christ, we become a part of the family of God—a member of his own household (Ephesians 1:5-6).

God makes them heirs of heaven

What earthly inheritance can compare with the inheritance God has in store for his children? In Christ, we will inherit the eternal kingdom of God. All the glories of heaven have been willed to us as God's children in Christ (1 Pet. 1:3-6).

These are the "what" that inform the "how." Faith and baptism are the means through which we help people come into the full experience of these amazing gifts from God. Thank God that you get to be a part of this wondrous work.

2 GETTING THE MESSAGE RIGHT

*E*vangelism is the sharing of the "evangel"—which is the good news. But what is the good news?

Focus on the basic story

One helpful way to think about the good news is to see it as a story (a true story!). The Bible's plot is centered on the good news. That story is summarized in four words: Creation, Fall, Redemption, Re-Creation.

Creation: God created the first man and woman to love, serve, and enjoy him forever.

Fall: Man sinned by choosing to defy God. In doing so, he forfeited the life and fellowship God had given him and mankind was thrust into a state of judgment and separation from God.

Redemption: Rather than banishing mankind from him forever, God promised to send a Redeemer who would pay the price for their sins and restore them to fellowship with God again. That Redeemer was Jesus—who was God Himself in human flesh. Jesus was born, died, and rose again from the dead to redeem all who would believe on him by faith.

Re-Creation: God will one day re-create the heavens and the earth and will restore the perfect world Man forfeited in the fall. In that recreation, there will be no more sin or death, and there will be eternal joy and blessing. Unbelievers, however, will experience eternal death and separation from God.

Memorize this story! Be able to tell it anywhere, anytime, to anyone, informally or formally. They will help you tell the good news faithfully and succinctly.

Be careful not to confuse people with mixed messages

It is easy to fall into some potholes when it comes to the good news. Be careful not to confuse people with mixed messages about what the gospel is about.

For example, the good news is not…

Johnny be good. The message we must share is not a "clean up your act and God will like you" message. Be careful of giving the impression that the good news is just moral improvement.

You can do it! Be careful of making the good news some form of a self-help message. For example, telling people that "God helps those who help themselves." While this quip may sound good, it's not in the Bible.

Whatever. Avoid affirming the idea that all religions are the same and all people are going to heaven. The good news is certainly available to all, but it is tied exclusively to Jesus Christ (John 14:6).

3 PROVEN WAYS TO SHARE THE GOOD NEWS

*I*f you have built a relationship with someone and are at the point where you can share the good news with them, you can do that in numerous tried and true ways. Try one of the following:

The ABCs of salvation

Simply share with people that becoming a follower of Jesus is as simple (Don't say easy!) as ABC.

> ***Admit*** *you have sinned.*
> ***Believe*** *on Jesus Christ.*
> ***Confess*** *Christ publicly.*

This method works great if you want to share the good news briefly. It works well with children and youth as well as adults. Consider printing out some bookmarks with the ABC of Salvation printed on them. You can give them away to people with whom you share the message.

You can see or download some sample bookmarks at: www.teenmissions.org/ABCBookmark.pdf

The Romans Road

The Romans Road is a terrific Scripture-based way to share the plan of salvation. This method walks people through passages in the book of Romans, answering key questions that lead to the good news of Christ.

I am a "good person," do I really need salvation?

...for all have sinned and fall short of the glory of God. (Romans 3:23)

As it is written:
"There is no one righteous, not even one..."
(Romans 3:10)

Therefore, just as sin entered the world through one man, and death through sin, and in this way death came to all people, because all sinned... (Romans 5:12)

I am not a bad person, is my sin really that bad?

For the wages of sin is death, but the gift of God is eternal life in Christ Jesus our Lord.
(Romans 6:23)

I am too bad to be saved. How can there be any hope for me?

But God demonstrates his own love for us in this: While we were still sinners, Christ died for us. (Romans 5:8).

How can I be saved?

If you declare with your mouth, "Jesus is Lord," and believe in your heart that God raised him from the dead, you will be saved. For it is with your heart that you believe and are justified, and it is with your mouth that you profess your faith and are saved.
(Romans 10:9-10)

Did God accept me?

…for, "Everyone who calls on the name of the Lord will be saved." (Romans 10:13)

Therefore, since we have been justified through faith, we have peace with God through our Lord Jesus Christ. (Romans 5:1)

Therefore, there is now no condemnation for those who are in Christ Jesus. (Romans 8:1)

For I am convinced that neither death nor life, neither angels nor demons, neither the present nor the future, nor any powers, neither height nor depth, nor anything else in all creation, will be able to separate us from the love of God that is in Christ Jesus our Lord.
(Romans 8:38-39)

One-verse evangelism

This method centers on one verse of Scripture to share the good news. The Scripture is Romans 6:23, *For the wages of sin is death, but the gift of God is eternal life in Christ Jesus our Lord.*

Share that verse, then highlight keywords and discuss them like this:

> **Wages:** People should get what they deserve.
> **Sin:** Sin is present in every person.
> **Death:** Eternal separation from God is the wage of sin.
> **But:** Thankfully, this unwelcome news is not the whole story.
> **Gift:** A gift is free but must be purchased.
> **Of God:** God has chosen to give us a gift instead of what we deserve.
> **Eternal life:** The gift God gives us is eternal life with him.
> **Jesus Christ:** The way we receive the gift is through trusting that Jesus died and rose again for us.

Conclude the presentation by asking if the person would like to receive the gift of salvation by praying to receive Jesus as their Savior and Lord (see sample prayers in Chapter 7).

One-Verse Evangelism by Randy D. Raysbrook, published by NavPress, provides a creative, visual way to present this message.

The Way of the Master

TV show hosts Ray Comfort and Kirk Cameron have developed an evangelism technique that focuses on confronting people with the Ten Commandments (Ex. 20: 1-17) as a way of helping them to acknowledge their guilt and their need for forgiveness and salvation.

This is a more confrontational approach to evangelism, but if done in love and gentleness, it can be an effective way to share the good news.

Begin by asking the person, "Do you consider yourself to be a good person?" If the person answers "Yes," then proceed to walk through some of the Ten Commandments like this:

How many lies do you think you have told in your life, including "white lies"?

Have you ever stolen something, even something little?

Have you ever misused the Lord's name?

Have you ever looked at a woman or a man with lust?

As the person answers in the affirmative to one or all these kinds of questions, then say, "In light of your own admission, if God were to judge you by the standard of the ten commandments, do you think you would be found innocent or guilty and would you be going to heaven or hell?"

Then take the opportunity to share the key elements of the good news, using the ABCs of Salvation or the Romans Road. Emphasize the person's need for repentance and faith.

Evangelism Explosion

Known also simply as EE, this method was popularized by James D. Kennedy (1930-2007), a long-serving pastor of Coral Ridge Presbyterian Church, Fort Lauderdale, Florida. The central approach of EE is to ask two assessment questions, which can then help lead to a faith conversation. Here is a slightly paraphrased version of these questions:

- Do you know for certain that if you died today, where you would spend eternity?
- If you died today and stood before God, how would you answer the question: "Why should I let you into heaven?"

Many older adults who grew up in the church may have received some training in EE or recall these questions. To explore or learn more about this approach, visit www.evangelismexplosion.org.

The bridge

Say to the person or group, "Imagine you're standing on one side of a large canyon, and your best friend is on the other side. You are separated by a giant chasm. How will you get across to where your friend is? You could try to jump. But even the most athletic person will not get far. What you need is a bridge that you can walk over."

Then say, "In the same way, we are separated from God by the chasm of sin. No amount of human effort can bring us to where God is. So, God has provided a bridge to connect us—Jesus Christ. He died for our sin and rose again from the dead, and he is the bridge that connects us back with God."

Conclude this simple presentation by saying, "Though the bridge has been provided, we must walk over it. We do that by simply placing our faith and trust in Jesus Christ." Ask the person if they would like to walk over that bridge today. Lead them in one of the prayers provided in Chapter 7.

Personal testimony—elevator version

A great lead-in to sharing the good news message is simply sharing how you came to experience the gifts of salvation yourself. If you were in an elevator with an unbeliever, riding from the first floor to the 10th floor, how would you share your personal testimony in such a short space of time?

Be prepared to highlight key details at any given moment. Share how you were lost in sin. Share how and when you received Jesus as your Savior and Lord. Then share the difference he has made in your life.

Here is how that elevator conversation may sound:

The unbeliever may ask, "Why are you carrying a Bible?"

You say, "It contains a message that changed my life."

The unbeliever says, "What do you mean?"

You say, "Until 10 years ago, I thought life was all about me. I hurt and disappointed a lot of people. But then a friend told me how Jesus came to die for my sins and give me a whole new life. I received him into my life. Now I live each day with the assurance of eternal life, and I find great purpose in loving and serving others."

Your testimony will accomplish one of two things. It may lead to more questions or a longer conversation. Or it may simply plant a seed that God will continue to water in the future. Either way, your brief testimony may be the conversation God uses to open the door of faith in another person's heart.

Personal testimony—long version

Sometimes there's the opportunity to share a longer version of your story. Share what your life was like before you came to receive Jesus, how and when you received him, and what your life is like now.

Emphasize more than the facts of your testimony (who, what, when, where). Share the emotions you experienced during these times. Explain how you felt lost, confused, or guilty. Share how Jesus came into your life and gave you peace, joy, and confidence. Tell how your life is now filled with hope and meaning as you live each day for the Lord.

Though it is *your* testimony, be sure it points to *Jesus*. Your testimony is like a pair of binoculars—it's meant to help people see Jesus more easily and clearly. Consider inviting people to pray to receive Jesus at the conclusion of your testimony.

4 INVITATIONS FROM THE PULPIT

*Y*our regular preaching ministry is one of the best evangelistic opportunities you have. Consider using one of the following ideas to invite people to receive Jesus from the pulpit (or lectern, or music stand, or whatever you use).

Provide a moment for silent prayer

At the end of your sermon, simply provide a few moments of silence and encourage people to speak to God personally. You can gently prompt this by saying, "Let God know what you're thinking and feeling today." Allow enough time for people to pray, but not so much that it feels belabored. Not all awkward silence is bad, but use it judiciously.

Give a gentle invitation

Say, "If you would like to talk to someone after the service about receiving Jesus as your Savior, I and/or others (elders, deacons) will be here at the front to talk to you." If someone comes, you could share the good news with them and pray with them. Be sure you have some literature to share with them (e.g., a gospel tract like the Billy Graham Evangelistic Association's "Steps to Peace With God").

Lead a guided prayer

At the end of the sermon or service, say, "If you would like to pray to receive Jesus, repeat this prayer in your heart as I pray it aloud." You can use one of the prayers in Chapter 7. Be sure to encourage people to communicate their decision in some way. They could share it with you, lift a hand, or fill out a card.

Give an altar call

At the end of your sermon or service, while the congregation is still present, you could ask people who would like to receive Jesus to get up from their seat and come to the front where you and other leaders can counsel them. It often works best to have the congregation or worship team sing a song during this time.

For many people, a physical, public response helps to cement the decision they are making. This is also a wonderful opportunity to surround new believers with prayer and support from the congregation. It also gives a chance for personal interaction and follow-up.

5 EVANGELISM EVENTS

*Y*our church could host events that encourage evangelism and sharing the good news. Think of these events as "top of the funnel" events. They are meant to be wide open to everyone. Here are some that have proven to be effective

Vacation Bible School

When you hold your VBS, consider presenting the gospel message in simple language for

the kids who attend. Or consider presenting the good news message to the families and friends who attend the closing service if you have one.

Kids clubs

You could hold a midweek Bible Club for children. This could be after school or in the evening. There are many programs you could utilize, such as Awana, Pioneer Clubs, Child Evangelism Fellowship, or one available from your denomination.

For children who otherwise do not go to VBS or Sunday School, some form of a midweek club may be a great way to connect with the kids in your community as well as their families. Be sure to regularly share the good news with the children who attend.

Special meetings

Whether you call them revival meetings, Bible conferences, crusades, campaigns, or spiritual emphasis retreats, special meetings are an effective way to share the good news. Invite a special speaker to speak on an interesting topic or to preach a series of evangelistic messages. Consider inviting a singer or band to lead worship during these meetings. The goal is to encourage people to invite unbelievers to these meetings. Consider giving an invitation to receive Christ at each of the meetings.

A key to effective special meetings is promotion. Get the word out as far in advance as you can. Make flyers, posters, and invitations. Consider sending out a special mailing. Advertise on the radio, your website, and social media. Do not skimp on the promotion! It will make all the difference.

Testimonial services

Have a special service where you ask several people to share their

personal testimony. It may be the testimony of their salvation or what God has done in their life. Follow up the testimonies with a presentation of the good news and an invitation to respond.

You could also consider showing a video of a celebrity or sports figure sharing their testimony. Or you could show an entire movie that shares the testimony of someone.

For example, the movie "I Can Only Imagine" tells the story of Bart Millard, who wrote the song "I Can Only Imagine." The story is not only about how the famous song was written but about how Bart's Father came to receive Jesus Christ before his death. Movies like this are a terrific way to share the good news with others in a fun and relaxing way.

Back to Church Sunday

The third Sunday of each September is National Back to Church Sunday. This is a concerted effort to invite people to attend church and for the church to provide a welcoming and encouraging environment for its visitors.

This is a time to share the love of Jesus and plant the seeds of the gospel in people's lives. Check out www.backtochurch.org for more information. Outreach has many great Back to Church Sunday resources. Check out www.outreach.com.

Christmas and Easter

Ah yes, the infamous two-times a year "Chreaster." We all know that Christmas and Easter services attract many people who otherwise do not attend church. Rather than being cynical about it, consider it a prime evangelism opportunity!

Sure, they may come to sing Silent Night and enjoy all the lilies decorating the church but be prepared to offer them much more. Be sure your Christmas and Easter services have a clear gospel presentation.

Share the message of the gospel in your message, in music, use media, or the arts. On Christmas, connect the dots between the cradle and the cross. On Easter, show the connection between the empty tomb and the cross. Whether you are talking about Jesus' birth or resurrection, be sure people hear about his death on the cross for them.

Invite people to receive Jesus in any of the ways mentioned in Chapter 3. However, because people are often in a hurry to leave these services to attend holiday get-togethers, encourage them simply to fill out a card that you can follow up later. Consider sharing the good news by distributing a booklet, tract, DVD, and/or link to online content at the exit doors.

As an extra bonus, arrange to have some of your church members available to take pictures of people in front of your church's Christmas tree or Easter decorations. Visitors will appreciate your extra hospitality, and it will give you one more opportunity to connect with visitors.

New members class

Offer a class that leads toward church membership. This could be a brief seminar or a weeks-long course.

Normally, church membership classes share with prospective members the beliefs, history, vision, mission, and ministries of the church. In addition, be sure to have a clear presentation of the gospel. Do not assume that someone who wants to join the church has embraced Christ as their personal Savior. The smaller group setting may be the perfect place for people to hear the good news message.

Use the opportunity to invite people to join *The Church*—Christ's Body—by receiving his gift of salvation. Then encourage them to join the local church.

As a part of the class, encourage new members to share their testimony either verbally or in writing. Consider adopting a policy that all new members must share their testimony of salvation with the spiritual leaders of the church (Pastor, Elders, Deacons). Build evangelism into your membership process.

Inquiry class or group

You could hold a special group or class for unbelievers to explore the Christian faith. This could be done in a home or in a classroom setting. An inquiry class presents the basic teachings of the Christian faith in a conversational, small-group atmosphere.

Some effective tools in this area include *The Alpha Course* (www.alphausa.org) and *Christianity Explored* (www.christianityexplored.com). These programs are designed to provide relational and non-threatening forums where people can bring their honest questions and find meaningful answers.

Confirmation

Many churches practice the confirmation of youth—often youth in middle school or early high school. Confirmation is meant to teach young people the basic truths of the Christian faith (often in the form of a catechism), together with introducing them to the contents of the Bible, church history, and encouraging them to put their faith into practice in service and mission.

Confirmation is often a path to receiving communion and church membership. However, confirmation can also be an evangelism event. Like membership classes, you can take the opportunity to share the simple gospel message with your students and invite them to respond.

Ask each student to write their testimony and share it on Confirmation Sunday. Some churches have students share their testimonies in a service the week before Confirmation Sunday.

For an added twist, consider adapting the content for adults and occasionally offer an adult option. This is one way to reach a growing number of adults who may be in your congregation or in the sphere of influence of your church who didn't grow up going to Sunday school or VBS.

Funerals and weddings

Include a brief gospel presentation at funerals and weddings. You may be surprised at the response you get! In both cases, people are in the church listening to you who may otherwise never come and listen. Make the most of it!

At funerals, do not just eulogize--evangelize! While people are confronted with the reality of death and the brevity of life, share the way to eternal life in Jesus.

Share the ABCs of Salvation or The Bridge illustration as a part of your message. Invite people to talk to you after the service if they want to learn more. So, stick around if you can. Talk to people after the service. Your message may have touched someone's heart, and they want to tell you about it.

At weddings, you can use the illustration of marriage to share the gospel. As you celebrate the love of the happy couple, share how Christ loved the church and gave himself for her (Eph. 5:25). Share that just these two individuals love one another, "God so loved the world that He gave His one and only Son…" (John 3:16). Think of a wedding as a living illustration of the gospel.

6 SCRIPTURES TO KNOW

*H*ere is a set of short Bible passages you could use in sharing the good news. This list is adapted from Intervarsity (https://ism.intervarsity.org/resource/13-bible-passages-share-gospel). Committing these verses along with those in Chapter 3 will add to your repertoire of evangelistic verses to know and use.

Creation: very good

For in him all things were created: things in heaven and on earth, visible and invisible, whether thrones or powers or rulers or authorities; all things have been created through him and for him. (Colossians 1:16)

God saw all that he had made, and it was very good. (Genesis 1:31a)

People: not so good

We all, like sheep, have gone astray, each of us has turned to our own way; and the Lord has laid on him the iniquity of us all. (Isaiah 53:6)

…for all have sinned and fall short of the glory of God… (Romans 3:23)

God sent His Son

For so loved the world that he gave his one and only Son, that whoever believes in him shall not perish but have eternal life. (John 3:16)

Jesus' authority

"But I want you to know that the Son of Man has authority on earth to forgive sins." So he said to the paralyzed man, "Get up, take your mat and go home." Then the man got up and went home. (Matthew 9:6-7)

"I and the Father are one." (John 10:30)

Jesus' nature

Who, being in very nature God, did not consider equality with God something to be used to his own advantage; rather, he made himself nothing by taking the very nature of a servant, being made in human likeness. And being found in appearance as a man, he humbled himself by becoming obedient to death—even death on a cross! (Philippians 2:6-8)

Jesus' resurrection

For what I received I passed on to you as of first importance: that Christ died for our sins

according to the Scriptures, that he was buried,
that he was raised on the third day according to
the Scriptures, and that he appeared to Cephas,
and then to the Twelve. (1 Corinthians 15:3-5)

Forgiveness

If we confess our sins, he is faithful and just and
will forgive us our sins and purify us from all
unrighteousness. (1 John 1:9)

Assurance of salvation

If you declare with your mouth, "Jesus is Lord,"
and believe in your heart that God raised him
from the dead, you will be saved. For it is with
your heart that you believe and are justified,
and it is with your mouth that you profess your
faith and are saved. (Romans 10:9-10)

Saved by the grace of God

For it is by grace you have been saved through
faith—and this is not from yourselves, it is the
gift of God—not by works, so that no one can
boast. (Ephesians 2:8-9)

Citizens and family

Consequently, you are no longer foreigners and
strangers, but fellow citizens with God's people

and also members of his household, built on the foundation of the apostles and prophets, with Christ Jesus himself as the chief cornerstone. (Ephesians 2:19-20)

Heaven

After this I looked, and there before me was a great multitude that no one could count, from every nation, tribe, people and language, standing before the throne and before the Lamb. (Revelation 7:9a)

7 PRAYERS OF SALVATION

The most meaningful prayers are those that spring from your own heart. That said, here are some sample prayers to provide you with examples and language you might find helpful in several instances.

A biblical prayer of a sinner (as relayed by Jesus)

Luke 18 contains the prayer of the tax collector, as told by Jesus. This parable shows that heartfelt repentance is much more important than the formula of words.

> *"But the tax collector, standing far off, would not even lift up his eyes to heaven, but beat his breast, saying, 'God, be merciful to me, a sinner!'"* (Luke 18:13)

Prayer for forgiveness

> *Dear God,*
>
> *I know I am a sinner. I know my sin deserves to be punished. Christ died for me and rose from your grave. I trust Jesus alone as my Savior. Thank you for the forgiveness and everlasting life I now have.*
>
> *In Jesus' name, amen.*

Sinner's Prayer for children

Jesus,

I know that you made me and want me to obey you with all my heart. I know I have disobeyed and wanted to be my own boss. I have thought and done things against your directions. I am sorry. I know that you gave up his life to save me from these sins and make me your child again. I accept your promises and ask you to please save me now and forever.

Amen.

Billy Graham's version of the Sinner's Prayer[1]

Dear God,

I know that I am a sinner. I want to turn from my sins, and I ask for Your forgiveness. I believe that Jesus Christ is Your Son. I believe He died for my sins and that You raised Him to life. I want Him to come into my heart and take control of my life. I want to trust Jesus as my Savior and follow Him as my Lord from this day forward.

In Jesus' name, amen.

---

1   From *Steps to Peace With God*, Billy Graham Evangelistic Association, PeaceWithGod.net/peace.

Campus Crusade for Christ salvation prayer[2]

Lord Jesus, I need You. Thank You for dying on the cross for my sins. I open the door of my life and receive You as my Savior and Lord. Thank You for forgiving my sins and giving me eternal life. Take control of the throne of my life. Make me the kind of person You want me to be.

Greg Laurie's salvation prayer[3]

Dear Lord Jesus,

I know I am a sinner. I believe You died for my sins. Right now, I turn from my sins and open the door of my heart and life. I confess You as my personal Lord and Savior. Thank You for saving me.

Amen.

---

2   From *The Four Spiritual Laws*, Bill Bright, Campus Crusade for Christ.

3   From Greg Laurie, *How to Know God*, www.harvest.org.

8 EVANGELISM PRO TIPS

Keep a prayer journal

*E*vangelism is more than technique. It is the work of God. Begin to pray for unbelievers that you may know. Print their names in a journal so you can remember them. Before you speak to people about God, speak to God about people.

You could purchase a special journal for your evangelistic prayer. Give each person their own page. Each time you pray for them, put a checkmark on the page. When he or she receives Christ, tear their page out and give it to them as a spiritual keepsake. Let them see your prayers for them.

Collect some useful resources

Gather your own trusted collection of evangelistic material you can easily give to people. Collect some booklets, pamphlets, tracts, DVDs, and other items you can give to people as the opportunity arises. Be sure to have some trusted websites you can point people to also. For example, www.exploregod.com is an excellent website to which you can refer unbelievers.

The resources you distribute should be substantial enough to present the gospel faithfully but not so substantial that they intimidate the person with whom you are speaking. Think of things that people can read or watch in a single sitting. Consider writing or stamping your name and contact information inside the resources that you distribute.

Carry business cards

Business cards are a simple and inexpensive way to connect with unbelievers, encourage further connection, and give people a "personal touch." You can give them to anyone, and they will not feel like you have just handed them a gospel tract.

If you want your cards to have an evangelistic element, consider printing a brief scripture verse on the back. For example, you could print Romans 10:9, "If you declare with your mouth, 'Jesus is Lord,' and believe in your heart that God raised him from the dead, you will be saved."

Study key topics

As you share your faith, you learn that unbelievers often raise similar issues. These include questions like, "If there is a God, then why so much suffering?" "What about people who have never heard about Jesus?" "Aren't all religions the same?" "How do you know the Bible is true?"

While you shouldn't feel the need to have answers for every question before you share your faith with others, it's a good practice to spend time studying biblical responses to common questions you're likely to be asked. Being prepared will help you be more conversant and better facilitate your evangelistic conversations. Consider spending time reading the many resources at www.exploregod.com. Their materials can help equip you to speak more confidently with unbelievers.

Get better at hospitality and "hygge"

Sharing Christ with others works best in the context of warm hospitality. Evangelism is much more natural and personal when you invite people into your home, share a meal, engage in real conversation, get to know one another, and then look for the opportunity to share your faith with them.

Inviting people into your home does not need to be an elaborate affair. Too much "putting on the ritz" may make people feel uncomfortable and out of place. Think simple, casual, low-key, come as you are, conversational, and fun.

The Danish word *hygge* (pronounced hoo-gah) beautifully captures the essence of uncomplicated hospitality. It means *cozy* or *comfortable*.

Think of being by a crackling fire with friends on a cold, snowy evening. You share hot chocolate, friendly conversation, and joyful laughter. That's *hygge*.

People love to experience coziness, and it creates an environment for sharing your faith. You want people to experience the warmth of Christ's love as they hear about the extent of Christ's love.

Be sure to send a small gift home with your guests. A scented candle is a great gift because it lasts, and when they smell it, they will remember their special time with you.

Make connections with seekers and skeptics

Be careful of becoming so much of a bookworm that you are no longer a "fisher of men." Many pastors enjoy prolonged study, reading, writing, and spending time in the office. Studying is a good and necessary part of ministry. But do not neglect getting out of your study and getting out into the community where you can rub shoulders with unbelievers.

Let people see you in a different light than just in the pulpit. Let them see you at the gym or in the basketball bleachers. Let them see you at the local firehouse pancake and sausage supper or at the 4th of July parade. Let them see you participating in everyday life. These are times when you build relationships with unbelievers and begin to open doors to share the good news.

Remember, the more people know you, the more open they will be to listening to you.

Don't hesitate to share the good news with young children

Children are a part of the harvest field. Never be afraid to do some gospel farming in the lives of children. The younger you can begin, the better.

You can *cultivate* by praying for children, showing care for them and their families, and building loving relationships with them. Consider hosting a backyard fun day for some young families. You could play some children's games, prepare a craft for them to do, go on a nature hike, have a puppet show, or show a children's movie. Combine this with a child-friendly cookout or ice cream bar, and young families are sure to have a great time. Events like this are great ways to build bridges to children and their families.

You can *plant* and water seeds beginning to place the Word of God in their hearts. Start a Beginners class in your Sunday School (or on another day in the week). Begin an after-school Bible club. Hold a children's church time during the Sunday service. Host a vacation Bible school. If your church practices Confirmation, consider beginning a pre-confirmation class for younger children. Start a Bible memory program for young children. Start a scholarship to help pay for children to attend a Christian camp.

You can *harvest* by inviting children to pray to receive Jesus. If possible, include the child's parents in that important conversation. The ABCs of Salvation (presented above) is a helpful tool in leading children to receive Jesus. You could also give children a gospel bracelet made of different colored beads. Explain the meaning of each color. Black represents sin. Red represents Jesus' blood. White represents cleansing. Green represents growth. Yellow represents heaven. Though you should make the message simple, don't oversimplify it by leaving out the key points of the gospel.

Lead them in a simple prayer to receive Jesus as their Savior and Lord. Here is an example:

Jesus,

> *I know that you made me and want me to obey you with all my heart. I know I have disobeyed you and tried to be my own boss. I have thought and done things you have told me not to do. I am sorry. I know that you gave up your life to save me from these sins and make me your child again. I believe your promises and ask you to give me a new life. Help me to grow as your child.*
>
> *Amen.*

9 WAYS TO ENCOURAGE BAPTISM

It's not a given in all cases that new believers will automatically request that you baptize them. Baptism often must be encouraged by a pastor. You can encourage people to take the step of baptism in a number of simple ways.

Encourage baptism through personal relationship

If you have a close, one-on-one relationship with a new believer, look for an opportunity to encourage them to be baptized. Personal encouragement is often the best motivation to action in ministry.

You could simply ask the person, "Have you ever considered being baptized?" Or "Would you like to be baptized?" The person may not understand what that means or entails, so be prepared to share why being baptized is an important part of expressing their faith.

Encourage baptism through personal discipleship

When a person becomes a new believer, ideally, they would be discipled (instructed) by a pastor or other leader. In discipleship, leaders strive to ground new believers in the core beliefs and practices of the Christian faith in a structured way. This is one of the best ways to help ensure new believers get off to a strong start in their new relationship with Jesus Christ.

As part of that discipleship process, you can present the scriptural call to baptism and encourage people to pursue making this public profession of their faith.

Encourage baptism through teaching and preaching

Consider teaching a class or preaching a message on the topic of baptism. You could cover what baptism symbolizes in the Bible, how baptism is conducted in your church, and the role baptism plays in expressing their faith in Christ.

As a part of the class or message, offer the opportunity for people to sign up for an upcoming baptism event.

Encourage baptism through scheduled baptism events

There are two ways to schedule baptisms. First, you can schedule them as the need arises. If a person comes to faith in your church, you can schedule a baptism for them.

Second, you can schedule a group baptism event and encourage people to sign up. You simply pick a date and announce that you will be baptizing on that date. Anyone who is interested can sign up for baptism.

A helpful way to facilitate a baptism event is to offer a baptism instruction class beforehand, especially if you have not taught or preached on baptism recently. This gives you the opportunity to instruct them on the meaning of baptism and ensure that they have come to salvation in Christ.

Encourage baptism through…baptism

This is the easiest way to encourage baptism. When you baptize someone, take the opportunity to say, "If *you* would like to consider being baptized, I would love to talk to you about that. See me after service or call me, and we can help you take this same step of obedience."

Physically seeing people take the step of baptism is a great motivator for others to take the same step. Such invitations may be opportunities for evangelism, as those who desire to be baptized may or may not be believers. Either way, this creates an open door for some great pastoral conversation.

10 BAPTISM TRAINING

Offer different kinds of training

Some churches baptize people with no training. If they come to faith in Christ, they just baptize them at the earliest possible convenience.

This "no training" approach is modeled after the baptism of the Ethiopian Eunuch in Acts 8:26-40. After Philip helped lead the Ethiopian to faith in Christ, he baptized him immediately on the side of the road.

While expediency can be great, providing some degree of training is a way to help foster maturity in a new believer. When it comes to baptism, your goal should be to help people experience it with eyes wide open—fully informed and prepared.

Training can be as simple as a pastoral visit with a prospective candidate for baptism. In the context of that visit, walk them through some basic instructions about baptism.

You could also hold a baptism candidate seminar. This is a one-session course for a group of people where you guide them through the basics of baptism.

Another idea is to host a baptism course. Begin a small group of 3-4 sessions where you walk a group of candidates through the baptism training. This has the advantage of building relationships among the candidates, which will continue into their life in the congregation.

Ideally, you can practice more than one of these training ideas to give people options. Also, do not feel you (pastor) must do all this teaching yourself. This is a great area to recruit other leaders who enjoy encouraging new believers to help you teach and train.

Provide instruction on the meaning of baptism

This is the heart of baptism training. You may have specifics to share that are part of your church or denomination's core teachings on baptism. You may also want to teach people the adage that baptism is "an outward symbol of an inward grace." In other words, baptism symbolizes deeper spiritual and biblical realities such as:

Baptism symbolizes how the blood of Christ washes away our sins

> Then one of the elders asked me, "These in white robes—who are they, and where did they come from?" I answered, "Sir, you know." And he said, "These are they who have come out of the great tribulation; they have washed their robes and made them white in the blood of the Lamb. (Revelation 7:13-14)

+r development +Research

Baptism symbolizes our union with Christ's death and resurrection

> *We were therefore buried with him through Baptism into death in order that, just as Christ was raised from the dead through the glory of the Father, we too may live a new life.*
> (Romans 6:4)

Baptism symbolizes our new life and identity in Christ

> *Therefore, if anyone is in Christ, the new creation has come: The old has gone, the new is here!* (2 Corinthians 5:17)

> *For all of you who were baptized into Christ have clothed yourselves with Christ.*
> (Galatians 3:27)

Provide teaching on how you baptize in your church

Teach your church's mode of baptism. Churches and denominations often have a preferred or required mode of baptism. Some baptize by immersion. If that's your church's tradition, explain that they will be placed all the way underwater for a moment. This could take place in a baptismal pool in the church, in a temporary water tank, or in a lake or river if performed outdoors. Immersions can even be performed in a jacuzzi.

Be sensitive to anyone who may have a fear of going underwater, assuring them you will help them all the way through the baptism. You (along with baptism team volunteers) may even consider showing baptismal candidates how the baptism will happen and rehearse it with them.

Some churches and denominations baptize by pouring. If that is your tradition, explain to the baptismal candidates that you will be pouring a small amount of water on the top of their head. Remind them that though the amount of water is small, they will still be getting wet. In fact, many churches pour three times (as the name of the Trinity is spoken). They will need to be prepared for a wet head, shoulders, and most likely face.

In addition to letting baptismal candidates know what to expect in terms of how baptism is done in your church, you may want to take the opportunity to explain why baptism is performed "in the name of the Father, the Son, and the Holy Spirit" (Matthew 28:19).

On the practical side, be sure to remind everyone that no electronics are allowed in the baptism area. They should remove any jewelry that may be damaged if it gets wet. Discourage makeup and hair products for the baptism, as they may run and get in their eyes or in the water.

Teach your church's requirements of baptism. If your church has a policy or requirements for baptism, go over it with candidates during training. Verbally communicate anything that is in writing. If your church does not currently have a baptism policy, consider creating one. It helps to ensure all baptisms are carried out according to the beliefs and values of your church.

Strongly consider including baptism rehearsal in your training

Show, tell, and practice exactly what will happen on the day of baptism.

Show. Bring the candidates to the pool, font, or area that will be used for their baptism. Point out anything unique or special. Explain how it is used. If you have any photos or videos of others being baptized in the pool or font, show them to your candidates. Help them visualize themselves being baptized so they are more comfortable.

Tell. Talk the candidates through the baptism step by step. Tell them what to wear (this is covered in Chapter 11). Tell them how to enter the pool (no diving or cannonballs, please). Tell them what you will say and what you will be asking them to say. Tell them how you will be holding them. Tell them where the towels will be after. Tell them where to go when the baptism is complete. Assume they know nothing about how baptism works and work hard to help them understand.

Practice. If possible, practice the baptism. If you are baptizing by immersion, stand with the candidate in the exact position they will be in when you baptize them.

Three immersion options

There are several ways to immerse someone in baptism.

Have the person stand and lean back under the water

The person being baptized should hold their nose with their left hand and hold their left forearm with their right hand, or the opposite if they prefer.

Using this method, you should support the candidate by placing your left hand flat against the middle of their back and holding their arm above the middle of their chest with your right hand, or the opposite if you prefer. Gently lean the person backward into the water until their face is under the water. Then help them stand straight up again.

Have the person stand, but just bend their knees rather than leaning back

The person should still hold their nose. Put your hands on the person's shoulders or head. Gently guide them as they bend their knees until the head is completely under the water. If the baptismal is deep enough (relative to the height of the person being baptized), this can be a good option for people with bad backs or for a heavier person who may be concerned or self-conscious about being raised up out of the water by the baptizer.

Have the person sit and then lean forward into the water

Sit in the water with the candidate. Place your hands on the person's head or shoulders. Help the person slowly bend face-first until their head is underwater. This is a good method to use if you are baptizing in a shallow creek or stream.

In all these options, you would say, "I baptize you in the Name of the Father, the Son, and the Holy Spirit," while their head is above water, as you want them to be able to hear the words being spoken to them.

If pouring

Typically, those being baptized will stand next to you with their hands at their side. You will need to be closest to the water so you do not have to reach across them. You will cup your hand, dip it in the water and fill it, then pour the water on their head. Or you could use a small cup or a seashell instead of your hand.

You could pour once as you say the Name of the Trinity. Or you could pour three times – once as you say, "Father," once as you say, "Son," and once as you say, "Holy Spirit."

When you have practiced these important moments and your candidates are comfortable with the experience, you are ready for baptism day!

11 BAPTISM CLOTHING

Prepare the clothing you will wear to baptize

Set aside some special clothing you use for baptism. Avoid clingy clothing. Dark colors work best because they are less see-through. Wear clothes that will not rise or fall during baptism. Avoid wool and dry-clean-only clothing.

In addition to a decent pair of waders, consider investing in a baptismal robe that can be worn over any clothing. If you or your church are able, invest in a set of baptism robes to reuse for baptism candidates. White is the traditional color for a baptism robe. Robes help minimize "wardrobe malfunctions" and lend dignity and modesty to the baptism service (you really do not want someone showing up in a speedo or skimpy bikini).

If you utilize robes, here's a helpful trick: Have fishing weights sewn into the bottom hem of your baptism robes. That will keep them from rising during baptism.

You may want to invest in some waterproof shoes (beach shoes work well). If you regularly baptize in a lake, stream, or pond, consider acquiring some fishing waders from your local sports outfitter.

Also, invest in a set of white towels that can be used at all your baptism services. Laundering robes and towels after a baptism makes a great ministry for someone in the congregation, as well as having someone volunteer during baptisms for towel duty.

Help the candidates prepare what they will wear for baptism

If they are not wearing a baptismal robe, candidates should wear modest, loose-fitting clothes. They should also avoid clothing that rises (like dresses) or falls (like pantyhose or baggy sweatpants).

They, too, should avoid see-through clothing and clothing that cannot get wet. They could wear water shoes or remain barefoot if preferred. Tell them to bring a change of clothes for after, including dry underwear.

If they are wearing robes, be sure they fit properly and are clean. Consider pinning their names on the robes so they get the correct ones on baptism day. When the baptism is complete, be sure you appoint someone to collect the robes, launder them, and return them to the closet in which they are stored.

Show candidates where to dress and change

Make sure your candidates know where to dress and change before and after the baptism. Provide a full-length mirror if possible.

And towels. Do not forget the towels! Provide them for your candidates, and if possible—more than one per person. Towels are inexpensive and help the candidates feel cared for after this important moment in their spiritual life. Make sure they are fresh and clean—as in bleach clean.

Protecting the privacy and modesty of those changing is important. Make sure to have separate changing accommodations for men and women. For adults, you may also wish to have a male volunteer be an attendant for the men's changing area and a female volunteer for the women's changing area. The function of these volunteers is to help ensure that the baptismal candidates have privacy, as well as being available to assist with any last-minute issues that arise (help needed with a hair clip, holding onto someone's glasses for them, etc.)

Regarding children and their privacy, they should have their own separate boy and girl designated changing areas and be attended to by their parent or guardian.

12 PREPARING THE WATER

Clean the surfaces

*B*efore you fill the baptistery, you will want to clean its surfaces. Never use any detergents or chemicals to clean the baptistery surfaces. They can damage the finish and create soap foaming.

It is best to clean all surfaces with a mild solution of water with a small amount of chlorine bleach (about a tablespoon of bleach in a cup of water). Then use a clean, lint-free cloth dampened with the cleaning solution to wipe down surfaces. This will both clean and disinfect. Dry with another clean, lint-free cloth or allow to air dry.

Also, drain the baptistery when not in use. Stale standing water can breed bacteria and mold.

Fill with water

If using a baptistery, fill it waist-high with clean water. If using a tank or tub, fill it about halfway. If you fill it too full, the water will spill out when you enter it.

Be sure to allow enough time for the water to heat (presuming your baptistery is heated or you have a portable heater for it). Generally, a water temperature in the 80s is comfortable for most people. As always, safety first! Be sure that all electric cords and any external devices you may have used to heat the tank are safely put away before anyone enters the water.

Sanitize the water

The best way to sanitize the water is by adding one cup of household chlorine bleach to the baptismal waters. Slowly pour the bleach directly into the center of the water. If the baptistery has a circulation system, the sanitized water will circulate throughout the system, thoroughly sanitizing all the surfaces that meet the water. Chlorine bleach is a natural and safe sanitizer, used to disinfect public drinking water and swimming pools.

If you are baptizing by pouring, clean the font or bowl in the same way. Sanitize the surfaces with mild bleach water before filling it with water.

If you are baptizing in a river, lake, or other outdoor body of water, be sure it is safe and unpolluted. Be sure no debris, dead fish, or slime is floating near you. While conditions can change, it's worth scouting out ahead of time an accessible spot that is relatively clean and fresh.

13 SERVICE OUTLINE

*H*ere's a basic order of service for baptism you can use as a template:

Words of institution

Therefore, go and make disciples of all nations, baptizing them in the name of the Father and of the Son and of the Holy Spirit, and teaching them to obey everything I have commanded you. And surely I am with you always, to the very end of the age. (Matt. 28:19-20)

Address

Baptism is the outward and visible sign of an inward and spiritual grace. It signifies entrance into a new life of fellowship with Jesus Christ our Lord. As you are baptized with water, so may you also be baptized with the Holy Spirit.

Though the form has changed with the centuries, the essential and unchanging condition of baptism has been the faith and consecration of the believer. We welcome you as you come to make your confession of faith and receive this symbol (or sacrament) of cleansing and divine fellowship, as commanded by our Lord for all believers.

Questions of faith and commitment

Pastor: Do you believe in God the Father, infinite in wisdom, goodness, and love; and in Jesus Christ, his Son, our Lord, and Savior; and in the Holy Spirit who takes the things of Christ and reveals them to us?

Respondent: I do.

Pastor: Do you confess that you are a sinner in need of forgiveness and salvation, and do you receive Jesus Christ as your personal Savior and Lord?"

Respondent: I do.

Pastor: Will you strive to know and do the will of God as taught in the Holy Scriptures and to walk in the ways of the Lord?

Respondent: I will.

Prayer

Almighty and everlasting God,

Receive and sanctify with your Spirit this your servant, now to be baptized according to your words. May (name of the baptized) find in you his/her refuge, his/her strength, his/her wisdom, and his/her joy. Keep (name) faithful to you all the days of his/her life that he/she may one day come into your everlasting kingdom through Jesus Christ our Lord.

Amen.

Baptism

(*Name of baptism candidate*), I baptize you in the name of the Father, and of the Son, and of the Holy Spirit. Amen.

Baptize candidate

Then say:

> But now, this is what the LORD says—he who created you, Jacob, he who formed you, Israel: "Do not fear, for I have redeemed you; I have summoned you by name; you are mine. When you pass through the waters, I will be with you; and when you pass through the rivers, they will not sweep over you. When you walk through the fire, you will not be burned; the flames will not set you ablaze.
> (Isaiah 43:1-2)

Closing prayer

O God,

May the heart of your servant be set to obey your commandments and give to (*name*) your peace which the world can neither give nor take away.

In Jesus' name, amen.

Benediction

To him who is able to keep you from stumbling and to present you before his glorious presence without fault and with great joy—to the only God our Savior be glory, majesty, power, and authority, through Jesus Christ our Lord, before all ages, now and forevermore! (Jude 1:24-25)

The Lord bless you and keep you;
the Lord make his face shine on you and be gracious to you;
the Lord turn his face toward you and give you peace. (Numbers 6:24-26)

Amen.

14 SCRIPTURES AND PRAYERS

Scriptures related to baptism

The baptism of Jesus

Then Jesus came from Galilee to the Jordan to be baptized by John. But John tried to deter him, saying, "I need to be baptized by you, and do you come to me?" Jesus replied, "Let it be so now; it is proper for us to do this to fulfill all righteousness." Then John consented. As soon as Jesus was baptized, he went up out of the water. At that moment heaven was opened, and he saw the Spirit of God descending like a dove and alighting on him. And a voice from heaven said, "This is my Son, whom I love; with him I am well pleased." (Matthew 3:13-17)

John the Baptist

And so John the Baptist appeared in the wilderness, preaching a baptism of repentance for the forgiveness of sins. (Mark 1:4)

John reveals Jesus

I myself did not know him, but the reason I came baptizing with water was that he might be revealed to Israel." (John 1:31)

Repent and be baptized

Peter replied, "Repent and be baptized, every one of you, in the name of Jesus Christ for the forgiveness of your sins. And you will receive the gift of the Holy Spirit. The promise is for you and your children and for all who are far off—for all whom the Lord our God will call." (Acts 2:38-39)

The Corinthians baptized

Then Paul left the synagogue and went next door to the house of Titius Justus, a worshiper of God. Crispus, the synagogue leader, and his entire household believed in the Lord; and many of the Corinthians who heard Paul believed and were baptized. (Acts 18:7-8)

Wash away your sins

And now what are you waiting for? Get up, be baptized and wash your sins away, calling on his name. (Acts 22:16)

Buried with Christ in baptism

Or don't you know that all of us who were baptized into Christ Jesus were baptized into his death? We were therefore buried with him through Baptism into death in order that, just as Christ was raised from the dead through the glory of the Father, we too may live a new life. (Romans 6:3-4)

Baptized by one Spirit

For we were all baptized by one Spirit so as to form one body—whether Jews or Gentiles, slave or free—and we were all given the one Spirit to drink. (1 Corinthians 12:13)

Clothed with Christ

So in Christ Jesus you are all children of God through faith, for all of you who were baptized into Christ have clothed yourselves with Christ. (Galatians 3:26-27)

One baptism

There is one body and one Spirit, just as you were called to one hope when you were called; one Lord, one faith, one baptism; one God and Father of all, who is over all and through all and in all. (Ephesians 4:4-6)

Circumcision and baptism

In him you were also circumcised with a circumcision not performed by human hands. Your whole self-ruled by the flesh was put off when you were circumcised by Christ, having been buried with him in Baptism, in which you were also raised with him through your faith in the working of God, who raised him from the dead. (Colossians 2:11-12)

Prayers for the newly baptized

By way of example and prompts as you give thought to your own invocations, here are a couple sample prayers.

Heavenly Father,

We give you humble thanks that you have called us to the knowledge of your grace and have given us the gift of faith in you. Increase this knowledge and confirm this faith in (name). Give your Holy Spirit to him that he may be born again and be made an heir of everlasting salvation through Jesus Christ our Lord.

Amen.

Gracious Lord,

In your goodness, you have given us a place within your church and marked us with the seal of your love in baptism. We pray for (name) who has now dedicated herself to you in this holy ordinance. Enable her daily to fulfill her vows. May your fatherly love shine upon her earthly path. May the grace of the Lord Jesus abound unto every good work, and may your Spirit rest upon her, to guide and comfort and sanctify. Let her never grow weary in welldoing, but fight the good fight and lay hold of eternal life.

In Jesus' name, amen.

15 CELEBRATION AND FOLLOW-UP

Provide a certificate of baptism

*P*rovide a signed baptism certificate indicating the date and place of baptism. Make sure it is nice enough to be a keepsake. You want the certificate to reflect the importance of the occasion. Certificates are available at church supply retailers.

If someone in your church writes in calligraphy, ask them to fill in the certificate for you. This is a nice way to add a distinctive touch to the marking of this special occasion.

Enter baptisms in your official church records

Be sure to enter all baptisms in your church records, whether in a book or a computer database. Baptism dates are important records for personal and church use and even genealogy study.

Provide gifts

Consider purchasing gifts for all newly baptized believers. Gifts should help the person remember their baptism day. Ideas include a Bible, a devotional book, a cross, a seashell, or a picture frame.

If you know someone who embroiders, consider commissioning them to embroider some white handkerchiefs with the baptismal candidates' names and the date of their baptism. These can also be used to cover their nose when baptizing before being given to them as a memento.

Host a reception

Host a reception or meal after the baptism service and invite the whole church family to attend. Encourage church members to sign a poster board to give to the newly baptized. Take pictures for your church newsletter or website.

Related to the public posting of pictures, be sure to request and obtain proper permission from those photographed beforehand and be respectful of those who decline. In the case of minors, parental permission should be sought.

Send an anniversary card

Make a note in your calendar to send a card to the newly baptized on the one-year anniversary of their baptism or recruit a volunteer to do this. This is a great ministry opportunity, especially for someone who may otherwise be limited in what they are able to do and for those who have the gift of encouragement.

"Remember your baptism"

When you baptize someone, take an extra moment to remind everyone present to remember their baptism.

Take a hand full of water and let it fall back into the pool slowly (so they can hear the splash). As the water splashes say, "As you've witnessed this baptism today, remember your own baptism and the God to whom you belong."

16 BAPTISM PRO TIPS

Invite candidates to share a piece of their story

*D*uring the baptism, ask the candidates to share a brief part of their testimony. No need for long speeches, but a short public testimony is a wonderful witness.

Ask each one to share a life verse

Challenge each candidate to select a meaningful Bible verse they can share at their baptism, or you can relay it to the congregation on their behalf.

Say their name

When you baptize the candidate, say their name like this, "Tom Smith, I baptize you in the name of the Father, the Son, and the Holy Spirit."

Take pictures and video

Recruit someone in your church to take photos and videos of the baptism service and provide copies to the candidates.

Invite the congregation to participate

As part of the baptism service, ask the congregation, "Do you promise to love and support this person as a brother or sister in Christ? If so, say, 'We do.'"

If permitted in your church or denomination, consider allowing someone who was instrumental in the candidates' journey to faith in Christ to assist or participate in the baptism in some way. This can be as simple as having them be the one who hands a towel to the person exiting the baptistry.

Write a newsletter article

Recruit someone to author an article for your church newsletter or website featuring a brief bio of each of the newly baptized people.

A note about photos, should the article include them: Be sure to request and obtain proper permission of those photographed beforehand and be respectful of those who decline; and in the case of minors, parental permission should be sought.

Children can be baptized too

Recognizing that age guidelines vary by denomination and congregation, if permitted in your church, encourage children who receive Jesus as Savior and Lord to be baptized. As a rule, if you practice baptism by immersion, children should be potty trained and old enough to hold their breath underwater for at least three to five seconds before you baptize them.

One caveat: Do not baptize a child without first obtaining proper permission from the child's parent(s) or guardian. Have a time of instruction with the child and parents and practice the same way you would with an adult. You may even consider inviting the parents (or a parent, depending on what is practical in your setting) to enter the water with you and their child. This may help put the child at ease.

When baptizing children, consider either lowering the water level, or having a submersible block or stool in the baptistry upon which they can stand.

With children, count to the time of immersion: one-two-three. Instruct them that when you say three, they should take a big breath and hold it, close their eyes, and hold your arms tightly. Also, make sure they hold their nose closed or hold it closed for them. Consider offering them a swimmer's nose clip and goggles. Water in the nose and eyes is often the biggest mishap when baptizing children.

Children may have a harder time getting completely underwater during baptism. Leaning them back into the water is the easiest way to immerse children without having to apply pressure to dunk them. You may need to guide them down a little more firmly than an adult because they are lighter. Do not hold them underwater! Gently pull them back up as soon as they are immersed.

When they come up from the water, make sure to have a towel ready and have someone help them up out of the water. As with adults, make sure their clothing or robe is not rising or falling and that they know where to go to change in private.

If you baptize by pouring, consider making the water run down the back of their head rather than their face. This will help avoid getting water into their eyes.

May the Scriptures, prayers, and practical guidance in this handy little book be a blessing to you and your ministry!

About the Contributors

Author

John Fanella has been both a pastor and writer for the past 30 years. He and his family live in a parsonage in the bucolic countryside of western Pennsylvania. Beyond his pastoral heart and editorial talents, there are two things to know about John: He's a prankster and he's afraid of spiders.

General Editor

Matthew Lockhart spent more than twenty-five years serving in a variety of editorial and leadership roles in Christian publishing at Serendipity House, Group, and Standard/David C. Cook. With a penchant for book series development, he enjoys helping to create Kingdom-focused resources like the *ChurchLeaders Pastoral Pocket Guides*.